Contents

Meets **Accreditation Standard** for Child-created Bulletin Boards

Apples

2

Contents
Three Cheers for September 1–2, SV 9836-1

Introduction

This series of monthly activity books is designed to give first and second grade teachers a collection of hands-on activities and ideas for each month of the year. The activities are standards-based and reflect the philosophy that children have different styles of learning. The teacher can use these ideas to enhance the development of the core subjects of language, math, social studies, and science, as well as the social/emotional and physical growth of children. Moreover, the opportunity to promote reading skills is present throughout the series and should be incorporated whenever possible.

Organization and Features

Each book consists of seven units:

Unit 1 provides reproducible pages and information for the month in general.
- a newsletter outline to promote parent communication
- a blank thematic border page
- a list of special days in the month
- calendar ideas to promote special holidays
- a blank calendar grid that can also be used as an incentive chart

Units 2–6 include an array of activities for five theme topics. Each unit includes
- teacher information on the theme
- arts and crafts ideas
- a food activity
- poetry, language skills (songs, poems, raps, and chants), and books
- bulletin board ideas
- center activities correlated to specific learning standards (Language arts, math, science, social studies, and writing are included in each theme.)

Implement the activities in a way that best meets the needs of individual children.

Unit 7 focuses on a well-known **children's author**. The unit includes
- a biography of the author
- activities based on a literature selection
- a list of books by the author
- reproducible bookmarks

In addition, each book contains
- reproducible **icons** suitable to use as labels for centers in the classroom. The icons coordinate with the centers in the book. They may also be used with a work assignment chart to aid in assigning children to centers.
- reproducible **student awards**
- **calendar day pattern** with suggested activities

Research Base

Howard Gardner's theory of multiple intelligences, or learning styles, validates teaching thematically and using a variety of approaches to help children learn. Providing a variety of experiences will assure that each child has an opportunity to learn in a comfortable way.

Following are the learning styles identified by Howard Gardner.
- **Verbal/Linguistic** learners need opportunities to read, listen, write, learn new words, and tell stories.
- **Bodily/Kinesthetic** leaners learn best through physical activities.
- **Musical** learners enjoy music activities.
- **Logical/Mathematical** learners need opportunities to problem solve, count, measure, and do patterning activities.
- **Visual/Spatial** learners need opportunities to paint, draw, sculpt, and create artworks.
- **Interpersonal** learners benefit from group discussions and group projects.
- **Intrapersonal** learners learn best in solitary activities, such as reading, writing in journals, and reflecting on information.
- **Naturalist** learners need opportunities to observe weather and nature and to take care of animals and plants.
- **Existential** learners can be fostered in the early years by asking children to think and respond, by discussions, and by writing.

Gardner, H. (1994). *Frames of mind.* New York: Basic Books.

September News

Teacher: _____ Date: _____

Headline News

Coming Up

Happy Birthday to

Special Thanks to

Help Wanted

Three Cheers for September 1–2, SV 9836-1

September

Special Days in September

National Library Month Have children dictate a chart-sized thank-you letter to the local librarian and draw pictures from their favorite books. Then arrange a trip to the local library so children can deliver their pictures and letter.

Children's Good Manners Month Read *The Berenstain Bears Forget Their Manners* by Stan and Jan Berenstain. Then discuss the importance of good manners in school.

Labor Day Labor Day is the first Monday in September. Have children research the history of Labor Day on the Internet.

Grandparent's Day This day is the first Sunday after Labor Day. Have children plan a reception or tea and invite their grandparents. Then have children complete the activity master on page 9.

8 Jack Prelutsky's Birthday Read some poems by Jack Prelutsky in honor of his birthday.

11 Patriot Day Discuss the meaning of *patriot*. Display an American flag. Discuss the colors and patterns children see. Then talk about the meaning of the flag.

16 Collect Rocks Day Take children on a walk around the school grounds and invite each child to find one interesting rock. Provide art supplies for them to make a rock creature.

16 H.A. Rey's Birthday Have children celebrate with activities from the Author Study unit that begins on page 86.

17 National Apple Dumpling Day Have children flatten a biscuit and scoop a spoonful of apple-pie filling on one half of it. Help them fold the dough and seal it. Bake the "dumpling" according to the directions on the biscuit can and eat the treat for a snack.

19 National Butterscotch Pudding Day Have children help make butterscotch pudding and eat it for a snack.

21 or 22 Fall Take the children on a walk around the school and point out signs of fall. Invite children to draw a picture of something they saw. Then have them write a sentence to go along with their picture. Have them complete the activity master on page 10.

22 National Dear Diary Day Choose a book that is written in a diary format and read it to children. Then have them write a diary entry about something they have done during the day.

26 Johnny Appleseed Day Have children celebrate with activities from the Apples Aplenty unit that begins on page 71.

Three Cheers for September 1–2, SV 9836-1

September

Sunday	Monday	Tuesday	Wednesday	Thursday	Friday	Saturday

Three Cheers for September 1–2, SV 9836-1

Using the Calendar for Basic Instruction in the Classroom

Use the calendar-related games and activities on this page to practice math skills.

Word Problems Practice problem solving by asking children to use the calendar to answer a question. For example: It rained all week except on Monday, Wednesday, and Thursday. On which days did it rain?

Graphing Make a line graph to hang on the wall. Write the numbers 1–6 on the vertical axis and the twelve months of the year on the horizontal axis. Find out how many children have a birthday in each month and record on the graph. Connect the points to finish the line graph or have the children copy the data and make individual line graphs.

Patterning Have children color three days in the middle of the calendar red, yellow, and green. Then, have them color all of the remaining days using the same pattern. They will be extending patterns forward and backward.

Math Facts Make a large calendar page on a plastic tablecloth and lay it on the floor. Select a number that the children need to practice with addition, subtraction, multiplication, or division facts, for example, subtracting the number 9. Give players one beanbag each and have children take turns tossing the beanbag on the calendar. Each player will subtract the number 9 from the number that the beanbag lands on and write the equation.

Coin Values Assign a coin value to consonant letters and a coin value to vowel letters. Using the assigned values, have children total the value of each of the days of the week or the months of the year. Challenge them to find out which is worth more or less or compare one to another.

Estimation Select a specific unit of study, such as seeds. Have children estimate how many days it will take for a seed to sprout. Have them record their prediction on a calendar. Then have them record the actual day it sprouted and compare it to the estimated day.

Distances on a Number Grid Give children a calendar page of your choice. Have them find how many spaces they move from one number to another number. Example: How many spaces do you move to go from 17 to 23?

Special Days Additional activities for the special days below are on pages 9 and 10.

Grandparent's Day was originated by Marian McQuade, a housewife from West Virginia. She wanted to bring attention to lonely elderly people in nursing homes. In 1978, President Jimmy Carter proclaimed National Grandparent's Day would be the first Sunday after Labor Day. It was first celebrated in 1979.

First Day of Fall officially begins in the Northern Hemisphere on September 22, the Autumn Equinox. The Autumn Equinox is when there are twelve hours of daylight and twelve hours of night. Gradually the days get shorter and the nights get longer. The temperature begins to get cooler. These are nature's signs to plant and animal life to begin to prepare for winter.

Name _____ **Date** _____

Grandparent's Day

September						
S	M	T	W	T	F	S
		1	2	3	4	5
6	7	8	9	10	11	12
13	14	15	16	17	18	19
20	21	22	23	24	25	26
27	28	29	30			

Directions: Use the calendar to answer the questions.

Grandparent's Day is in September. It is the first Sunday after Labor Day. Labor Day is on the first Monday in September.

1. What is the date of Labor Day? _____

2. What is the date of Grandparent's Day? _____

3. Juan made a card for his grandparents on September 5. He mailed it 3 days later. On which date did he mail the card? _____

Unit 1, Teacher Resources: Activity Master
Three Cheers for September 1–2, SV 9836-1

Name _____   **Date** _____

Seasons: Fall

Directions: Use the calendars to answer the questions.

September						
S	M	T	W	T	F	S
		1	2	3	4	5
6	7	8	9	10	11	12
13	14	15	16	17	18	19
20	21	22	23	24	25	26
27	28	29	30			

October						
S	M	T	W	T	F	S
				1	2	3
4	5	6	7	8	9	10
11	12	13	14	15	16	17
18	19	20	21	22	23	24
25	26	27	28	29	30	31

November						
S	M	T	W	T	F	S
1	2	3	4	5	6	7
8	9	10	11	12	13	14
15	16	17	18	19	20	21
22	23	24	25	26	27	28
29	30					

December						
S	M	T	W	T	F	S
		1	2	3	4	5
6	7	8	9	10	11	12
13	14	15	16	17	18	19
20	21	22	23	24	25	26
27	28	29	30	31		

1. Fall begins on September 22. Which day of the week does fall begin?_____

2. What is the date 10 days after fall begins?

_____

3. The last day of fall is December 20. How many days are left in the year after December 20?

_____

Unit 1, Teacher Resources: Activity Master
Three Cheers for September 1–2, SV 9836-1

Our Fabulous Five Senses

 We could not function as we do without the information that we receive through our five senses. The most effective way to receive this information is to use all of the senses together.

 There are people who do not have the use of all five senses, but one sense can compensate for another in some instances. For example, if the sense of hearing is lost, the sense of sight can be used to read lips.

 All during our waking hours, our eyes are working like video cameras. Vision occurs when light is processed by the eye and interpreted by the brain.

 Taste buds are sensory organs that are found on the tongue. These taste buds allow you to experience tastes that are sweet, salty, sour, and bitter.

 Our nose has olfactory receptors that work together with the taste buds to create the true flavor of foods and then sends this message to the brain.

 Olfactory receptors allow you to smell thousands of different odors that may be pleasant or unpleasant and even odors that may warn of danger.

 The average person has about 10,000 taste buds. They are replaced every two weeks or so. As a person ages, these taste buds are not always replaced. Therefore, an older person's sense of taste is weaker than a younger person's sense of taste.

 The skin is the main organ of the sense of touch. The nerve endings in the skin can detect pressure, pain, and temperature.

 The ability to sense pain and temperature is a safety feature, but it also allows you to tell the difference between textures, or between wet and dry.

 The ear is the organ that provides hearing and balance. It consists of three parts which are the outer, the middle, and the inner ear.

 The outer and middle ear mostly collect and transmit sound, while the inner ear analyzes sound waves and contains an apparatus that maintains the body's balance.

 All of our five senses are important, but the sense of sight can easily be damaged or lost if safety precautions are not used.

Three Cheers for September 1–2, SV 9836-1

"Name" Textures

Materials

- poster board
- glue
- markers
- plastic containers
- scissors

- materials such as beans, cotton balls, rice, buttons, small candies, or small stickers

Directions

Teacher Preparation: Place the various materials in separate containers. Cut the poster board into four-inch strips. Write each child's name using large letters on pieces of poster board that correspond to the length of his or her name.

1. Trace the letters in your name with glue, one at a time.

2. Cover each letter with a different material. Allow it to dry thoroughly.

3. Close your eyes and try to "read" each other's names using only your sense of touch.

Five Senses Mobile

Materials

- patterns on page 20
- construction paper
- crayons or markers

- scissors
- hangers

- yarn
- hole punch

Directions

Teacher Preparation: Duplicate a copy of the five senses patterns on construction paper for each child.

1. Color and cut out the eye, ear, hand, nose, and tongue patterns.

2. Write the corresponding name of the sense on the back of each pattern.

3. Punch a hole in the top of each pattern piece.

4. Tie a piece of yarn through each hole. Vary the lengths of the yarn.

5. Attach the opposite end of each piece of yarn to a hanger to complete the mobile.

6. Hang mobiles from the ceiling to display.

A Taste and a Half

You will need

- pretzel sticks
- whole sour pickles
- marshmallows
- paper plates
- plastic knives

Directions

Teacher Preparation: Provide each child with an even number of pretzels and marshmallows and one whole pickle.

Lead a discussion with children about the taste buds that allow them to taste sweet, sour, salty, and bitter.

1. Divide each food item into halves. Use a plastic knife to cut the pickle in half.

2. Eat half of one food and identify the taste (salty, sour, or sweet).

3. Repeat with remaining food items.

4. Eat the remaining half of each food.

🎵 We Use Five Senses

(Tune: "Bingo")

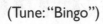

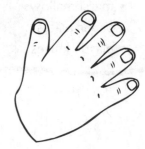

We use five senses when we play,

Each and every day.

See, smell, hear, taste, touch.

See, smell, hear, taste, touch.

See, smell, hear, taste, touch.

We use these when we play!

Use Your Senses to Enjoy These Stories

The Five Senses
by Keith Faulkner (Cartwheel Books)

The Indoor Noisy Book
by Margaret Wise Brown (HarperCollins)

Is It Rough? Is It Smooth? Is It Shiny?
by Tana Hoban (Greenwillow)

The Listening Walk
by Paul Showers (HarperTrophy)

Magic School Bus Explores the Senses
by Joanna Cole (Scholastic)

My Five Senses
by Aliki (HarperCollins)

You Can't Smell a Flower with Your Ear
by Joanna Cole (Grosset & Dunlap)

You Can't Taste a Pickle with Your Ear
by Harriet Ziefert (Blue Apple Books)

Three Cheers for September 1–2, SV 9836-1

Rolling Along with Our Five Senses

Materials

- pattern on page 21
- craft paper
- white construction paper
- border
- 8–9 inch paper plates
- stapler
- scissors
- markers
- brads

Directions

Teacher Preparation: Duplicate a copy of the wheel pattern on construction paper for each child. Cover the bulletin board with craft paper.

1. Write a word to complete each sentence on the wheel.

2. Draw a picture to illustrate each word.

3. Cut out the wheel.

4. Color the edge of a paper plate with a black marker to resemble the tire on a wheel.

5. Attach the wheel to the center of a paper plate with a brad.

6. Staple the wheels in a pleasing arrangement on the bulletin board.

7. Add a border and the caption.

Three Cheers for September 1–2, SV 9836-1

Our Fabulous Five Senses Centers

Art Center

Language Arts Standard
Correctly spells frequently used words

The Colors of the Rainbow

Materials

- construction paper
- round, multicolored, multigrain cereal
- glue

Invite children to glue round cereal on construction paper to make a rainbow. Have them use all five senses as they complete the picture. They can see, touch, smell, and taste the cereal. Challenge them to think of a way that they can use their ears during this project. For example, they can crunch cereal and hear the sound.

Extension: Have children write the corresponding color word next to each row of cereal.

Language Center

Language Arts Standard
Uses sound-letter relationships and phonics as word recognition strategies

Which Sense Is It?

Materials

- activity master on page 22
- crayons

Teacher Preparation: Duplicate a copy of the activity master for each child.

Invite children to name the five senses. Then have them circle the words that answer each question and color the pictures.

Our Fabulous Five Senses Centers

Science Center

Science Standard
Collects data gained from direct experience and records on individual charts

What Is That Scent?

Materials

- activity master on page 23
- one package each of orange, strawberry, watermelon, and grape powdered drink mix
- four empty yogurt containers with lids
- black marker
- scissors

Teacher Preparation: Duplicate an activity master for each child. Pour one package of each powdered drink mix into each of the four yogurt containers and place the lids on top. Poke several holes in the lids. Write a number from 1 to 4 with the black marker on each container.

Tell children they are going to use their sense of smell to identify flavors of powdered drink mix. Invite them to shake container 1 to release the scent and smell it. Have children use the word box at the top of the page to name the smell. Challenge them to write the name of the smell to complete the sentence. Repeat with containers 2–4.

Game Center

Language Arts Standard
Uses information from what they have learned to develop vocabulary

Five Senses Word Puzzle

Materials

- activity master on page 24

Teacher Preparation: Duplicate a copy of the activity master for each child.

Invite children to use the clues that relate to the five senses and find the answers in the word box. Have them write the answers in the puzzle.

Our Fabulous Five Senses Centers

Math Center

The Eyes Have It

Materials

- activity master on page 25
- scissors
- white craft paper
- crayons
- glue
- tape

Teacher Preparation: Duplicate a copy of the activity master for each child and three extra eye patterns. Tape a large piece of craft paper on the wall and draw lines to form three columns. Cut out the extra three eye patterns and color one blue, one brown, and one green. Glue one pattern at the top of each column to form a graph.

Invite children to color the eye pattern to match their eye color and complete the sentence. Then have them cut out the pattern and glue it in the appropriate column on the graph. Have children answer the questions using the completed graph.

Social Studies Center

The Three Bears Use Five Senses

Materials

- white craft paper
- markers
- tape
- a version of *Goldilocks and the Three Bears*

Teacher Preparation: Tape a piece of craft paper on the wall. Draw a large story web with five circles extending from the middle. Draw the Three Bears in the center of the web. In each of the five circles write the name of one of the five senses.

Read to children or have children read *Goldilocks and the Three Bears*. Invite children to draw or write on the story web how Goldilocks or the Three Bears used the five senses in the story. For example, the Three Bears saw the broken chairs. Have children draw a broken chair on the sight part of the story web.

Our Fabulous Five Senses Centers

Writing Center

Language Arts Standard
Identifies and writes simple sentences

A Noisy Place

Materials

- activity master on page 26
- *The Indoor Noisy Book* by Margaret Wise Brown
- crayons

Teacher Preparation: Duplicate a copy of the activity master for each child.

Read to children or have children read *The Indoor Noisy Book*. Discuss the noises that the dog heard in the house. Invite children to think of a place where there might be noises such as a farm, the classroom, or a circus. Have them write a sentence describing an object and the sound it makes. For example, they can write, "A pig goes oink, oink." Then have them illustrate their sentence.

Tip: Any of the noisy books by Margaret Wise Brown can be used for this activity.

Technology Center

Technology Standard
Uses proper keyboarding techniques

Making "Sense" of the Keyboard

Materials

- computer
- index cards
- marker

Teacher Preparation: Make word cards of the five senses for younger children.

Invite children to spell the names of each of the five senses on the keyboard. Encourage older children to write sentences using the five senses. For example, they can write, "I can see a pretty rainbow."

Five Senses Patterns
Use with "Five Senses Mobile" on page 12.

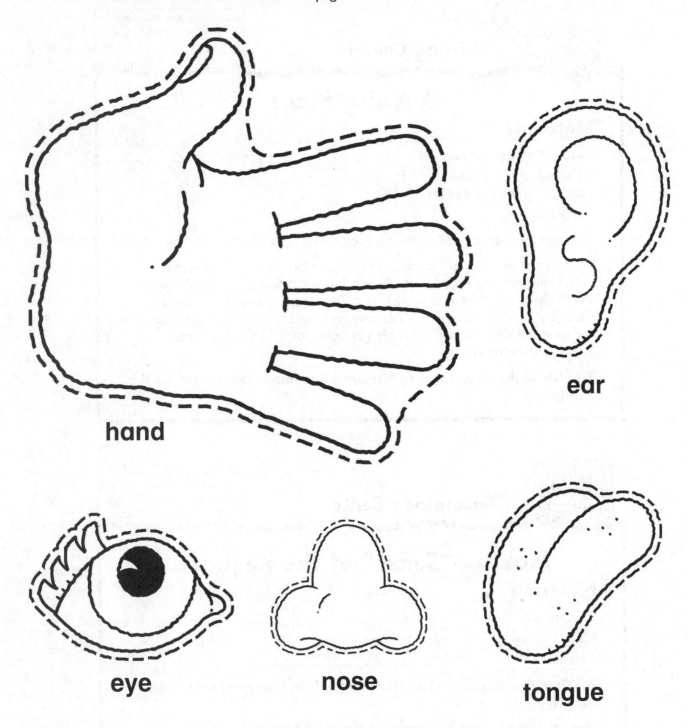

hand

ear

eye

nose

tongue

Unit 2, Our Fabulous Five Senses: Patterns
Three Cheers for September 1–2, SV 9836-1

Wheel Pattern

Use with "Rolling Along with Our Five Senses" on page 15.

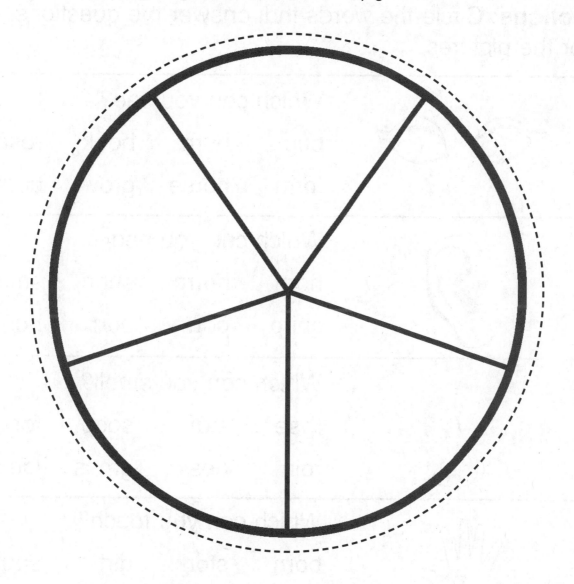

I can see _____.

I can hear _____.

I can taste _____.

I can smell _____.

I can touch _____.

Name _____ **Date** _____

Five Senses

Directions: Circle the words that answer the questions.
Color the pictures.

1	**Which can you see?**
	bug burn book rose
	form horse grow barn
2	**Which can you hear?**
	horn harm snarl smart
	chirp part purr harp
3	**Which can you smell?**
	rose star soap fork
	rain desk grass lamp
4	**Which can you touch?**
	born stork dirt spur
	sport bird shirt yarn
5	**Which can you taste?**
	tent fish yard corn
	gum flag brush bread

Use with "Which Sense Is It?" on page 16.

Unit 2, Our Fabulous Five Senses: Activity Master
Three Cheers for September 1–2, SV 9836-1

Identify the Scent

Directions: Shake each container and smell the scents. Use the word box to name each smell. Write the name of the smell in the correct box.

1	It smells like _____.
2	It smells like _____.
3	It smells like _____.
4	It smells like _____.

Use with "What Is That Scent?" on page 17.

Three Cheers for September 1–2, SV 9836-1

Name _____ Date _____

Word Puzzle

Directions: Read the clues and find the answer in the word box. Write the word in the puzzle.

radio	flower	rabbit	book	clock
ice	lemon	skunk	clap	stars

Across

3. a loud sound
5. smells nice
8. has words to see
9. see the time
10. see at night

Down

1. feels very cold
2. hear music
4. a bad odor
6. tastes sour
7. feels soft

Use with "Five Senses Word Puzzle" on page 17.

Unit 2, Our Fabulous Five Senses: Activity Master
Three Cheers for September 1–2, SV 9836-1

Name _____ Date _____

Eye Graph

Directions: Color the eye pattern to match your eye color.
Cut it out and glue it on the graph. Complete the sentence.
Look at the graph and answer the questions.

1. How many girls have brown eyes? _____

2. How many boys have blue eyes? _____

3. Which eye color did the most children have? _____

4. Which eye color did the least children have? _____

_____'s eyes are _____.

Use with "The Eyes Have It" on page 18.

Unit 2, Our Fabulous Five Senses: Activity Master
Three Cheers for September 1–2, SV 9836-1

Name _____ Date _____

Noisy

Directions: Draw a picture of something that makes a sound. Write a sentence telling about the sound it makes.

_____

_____.

Use with "A Noisy Place" on page 19.

Three Cheers for September 1–2, SV 9836-1

Check Out Your Community

 A community is a place where people live and work. The people in each community can work together and thus have a positive influence on the community.

 There are different kinds of communities such as rural, suburban, and urban. Different communities require different things.

 Every community has the same basic needs. There is a need for air, land, garbage and sewage plants, a water supply, food and energy sources, schools, and stores.

 Some code of behavior is necessary for every working community. These laws are enforced by people who are trained in law enforcement.

 It is important that communities provide for the health and safety of the people who live there. Hospitals, fire stations, and police stations are located throughout each community.

 School is an important part of every child's community. The work of teachers, librarians, food workers, custodial workers, and many others all contribute to the success of the school community.

 Communities provide places for recreation and for learning. These places might include parks, a zoo, a library, and a museum.

 Communities are made up of producers and consumers. A producer is someone who provides a good or service for others. A consumer is someone who consumes a good or uses a service.

 Each community has its own history. Communities experience change as time goes by, and many face the challenges that come with growth.

Helper Puppets

Materials

- patterns on page 36
- white construction paper
- jumbo craft sticks
- crayons
- scissors
- glue

Directions

Teacher Preparation: Duplicate the community helper patterns on white construction paper. Enlarge patterns if desired.

1. Color and cut out the doctor, plumber, firefighter, and police officer patterns.

2. Glue each one to a craft stick.

3. Draw the face of another person that works in a community such as a baker with a baker's hat.

4. Color it, cut it out, and glue it to a craft stick.

Note: Use the puppets with "Community Helpers Puppet Show" on page 34.

Mapping Our School Community

Materials

- outline of the classroom
- map of the school
- ruler
- markers

Directions

Teacher Preparation: Provide a copy of the outline of the classroom and the map of the school for each child.

Lead a discussion with children about how maps symbolize real places and things.

1. Take a tour of the school using the map.

2. Draw and label the furniture in the classroom on the outline of the room.

3. Ask a friend to locate your desk or table on the map.

Three Cheers for September 1–2, SV 9836-1

Cookies for Sale

You will need

- ingredients for a favorite cookie recipe
- mixing bowls and spoons
- measuring cups and spoons
- cookie sheet
- oven
- poster board
- markers

Directions

1. Lead a discussion with children about how some people produce goods for the community, and how the money made from the sale of these goods can be used to help others.

2. Have children work as a class or in teams to bake the cookies.

3. Determine how much to charge for the cookies and make signs.

4. Arrange for a time and place for children to sell the cookies such as at lunch or after school.

5. Have children select a local charity to which they would like to donate the proceeds of the cookie sale.

6. If possible, take a field trip to the charity location and have children present the money.

7. Have children evaluate the project in a group discussion.

Three Cheers for September 1–2, SV 9836-1

♫ Let's All Look

(Tune: "Here We Go 'Round the Mulberry Bush")

Let's all look at the many jobs,
many jobs, many jobs.
Let's all look at the many jobs
All around (name of your city).

This is the way I check your ears,
check your ears, check your ears.
This is the way I check your ears
when you pay me a visit.

This is the way I make your bread,
make your bread, make your bread.
This is the way I make your bread
before it comes to your store.

This is the way I fly the plane,
fly the plane, fly the plane.
This is the way I fly the plane
so you get where you are going.

This is the way I sort the mail,
sort the mail, sort the mail.
This is the way I sort the mail
so you will get your letters.

This is the way I hold the hose,
hold the hose, hold the hose.
This is the way I hold the hose
so I put out the fire.

Invite children to learn the song and sing it in the communication center on page 34.

Communities Come Together in These Books

Big Frank's Fire Truck
by Leslie McGuire
(Random House for Young Readers)

Calling Doctor Amelia Bedelia
by Herman Parish (Greenwillow)

Come Back, Amelia Bedelia
by Peggy Parish (HarperTrophy)

Mapping Penny's World
by Loreen Leedy (Henry Holt & Co.)

Me on the Map
by Joan Sweeney (Dragonfly Books)

Town and Country
by Alice Provensen (Random House)

Wanda's Roses
by Pat Brisson (Turtleback)

Window
by Jeannie Baker (Greenwillow)

The Needs of a Community

Materials

- craft paper
- activity master on page 37
- crayons or markers
- list of local businesses
- construction paper
- stapler
- border

Directions

Teacher Preparation: Cover the board with craft paper. Provide a copy of the activity master for each child and post a list of local businesses.

Lead a discussion with children about the needs of a community such as food and clothing.

1. Complete the activity master.
2. Attach the activity masters to colorful construction paper and staple them in a pleasing arrangement on the bulletin board.
3. Add a border and caption.

Check Out Your Community Centers

Language Center

Language Arts Standard
Recognizes final consonants

Fun in Our Community

Materials

- activity master on page 38
- crayons

Teacher Preparation: Provide a copy of the activity master for each child.

Discuss with children the various places in the community where people go for recreation. Invite children to write the consonant that stands for the **last** sound of each fun activity.

Math Center

Math Standard
Writes number sentences using +, −, and =

Community Helpers Computation

Materials

- activity master on page 39

Teacher Preparation: Duplicate a copy of the activity master for each child.

Invite children to read the word problems and write a number sentence. Then have them add or subtract to solve the problems.

Check Out Your Community Centers

Social Studies Center

Social Studies Standard
Identifies ways people exchange goods and services

Community Helpers Concentration

Materials

- picture cards on page 40
- crayons
- poster board
- ruler
- construction paper
- scissors
- black marker

Teacher Preparation: Duplicate the picture cards on construction paper. Color, cut out, and laminate them for durability. Make a game board by cutting a 12-inch by 12-inch square of poster board. Divide it into 16 equal squares.

Invite partners to mix the picture cards and place them facedown on the game board. Then have them take turns turning over two cards. The cards can be removed from the board if the two cards are related such as a doctor and a stethoscope. Have children tell if this person provides a good or a service to the community. Tell children to turn the cards facedown on the game board if they do not match. Tell children to continue play until all pairs are removed from the board.

Science Center

Science Standard
Understands how weather affects what people wear

Weather Forecast

Materials

- weather reports from the newspaper
- crayons or markers

Discuss why it is helpful to know about the weather in advance. Have children use the newspaper to find the weather forecast for the next day. Invite children to draw pictures of themselves dressed appropriately for the next day's weather.

Check Out Your Community Centers

Communication Center

Community Helpers Puppet Show

Materials

- puppet patterns on page 36
- puppet stage

Invite children to follow the directions for making the puppets in "Helper Puppets" on page 28. Then have them learn the song in "Let's All Look" on page 30 and create a few additional verses. Encourage children to sing the songs in front of an audience using the puppets and a puppet stage.

Note: Arrange for a group of younger children to be the audience.

Literacy Center

Community History

Materials

- crayons
- historical materials about your community

Teacher Preparation: Place historical materials in the literacy center.

Provide children with information such as books, articles, or websites on the history of their community. Invite them to write a sentence or paragraph about something that they learned about the history. Then have them illustrate it.

Check Out Your Community Centers

Writing Center

Language Arts Standard
Uses word and letter spacing and margins to make messages readable

It's Off to Work I Go

Materials

- crayons

Discuss with children the various jobs that people do. Invite them to write a sentence or paragraph telling what job they would like to do when they are grown. Then have them illustrate it.

Game Center

Language Arts Standard
Uses structural cues to recognize words

Around the Community Word Search

Materials

- activity master on page 41

Teacher Preparation: Provide each child with a copy of the activity master.

Discuss with children the various jobs that people might do in a community. Invite them to circle the names of community helpers found in the word puzzle.

Stick Puppet Patterns

Use with "Helper Puppets" on page 28 and "Community Helpers Puppet Show" on page 34.

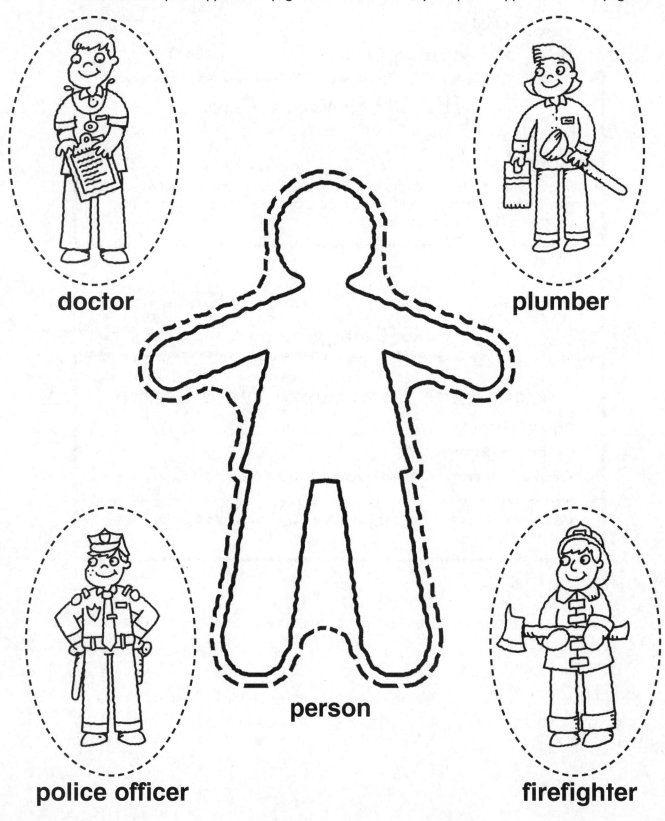

doctor

plumber

person

police officer

firefighter

Three Cheers for September 1–2, SV 9836-1

Name _____ Date _____

Meeting Your Needs

My name is _____.

I live in _____.

The name of my school is

_____.

We buy groceries at _____.

The trash is picked up
at my house on

_____.

My family buys clothes at

_____.

┌─────────────────────────────────┐
│   │
│   Here is a place I   │
│   go to have fun.   │
│   │
│   │
│   │
│   │
│   │
│   │
│   │
│   │
│   │
│   │
└─────────────────────────────────┘

Use with "The Needs of a Community" on page 31.

Community Fun

Directions: Name each fun activity. Write the consonant that stands for the **last** sound.

1.  cam____	2.  swi____	3.  hi____e
4.  swin____	5.  ska____e	6.  rea____
7.  socce____	8.  sli____e	9.  bow____

Use with "Fun in Our Community" on page 32.

Word Problems

Directions: Read each word problem. Write the number sentence. Then add or subtract to solve.

1.

The baker made 24 donuts.
He sold 11 donuts.
How many donuts did
he have left?

_____

2.

The city had 27 buses.
They bought 12 new buses.
How many buses did the
city have?

_____

3.

The veterinarian took care
of 11 cats and 16 dogs.

How many animals did he
take care of all together?

_____

4.

Pam bought 13 stamps
at the post office.
She used 5 stamps.
How many stamps did
she have left?

_____

Use with "Community Helpers Computation" on page 32.

Community Helpers Picture Cards

Use with "Community Helpers Concentration" on page 33.

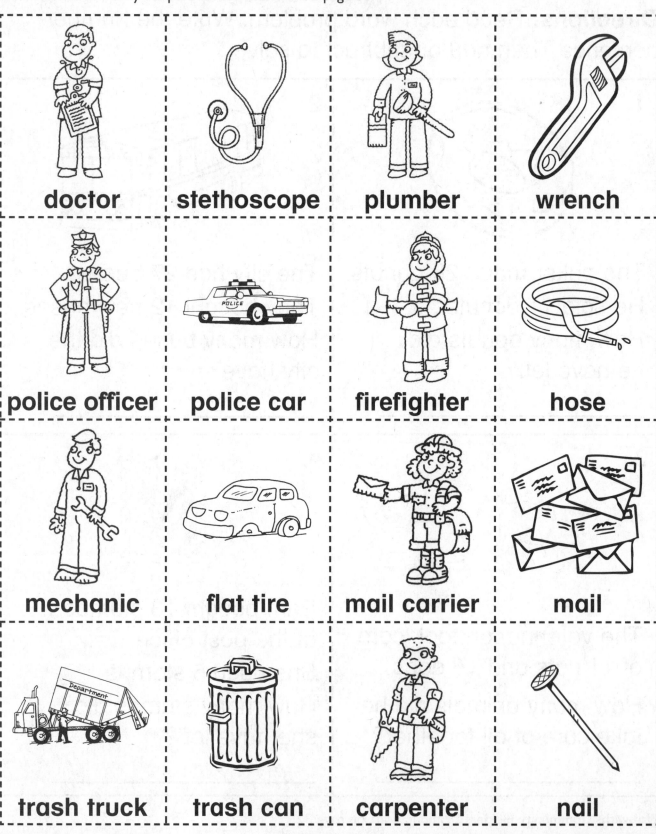

doctor	stethoscope	plumber	wrench
police officer	police car	firefighter	hose
mechanic	flat tire	mail carrier	mail
trash truck	trash can	carpenter	nail

Three Cheers for September 1–2, SV 9836-1

Name _____ **Date** _____

Word Search

Directions: Read the words in the box. Find each word in the puzzle and circle it. The words go across and down.

barber	carpenter	chef
clerk	doctor	farmer
grocer	mayor	nurse
plumber	police	teacher

g o c s e n d s f c

r t l m a y o r f e

o e e j s w c n a k

c a r p e n t e r n

e c k o m i o n m u

r h o l b a r b e r

o e c i d o c e r s

s r p c h e f s r e

z l l e n u b e k t

g f u p l u m b e r

Use with "Around the Community Word Search" on page 35.

Unit 3, **Check Out Your Community: Activity Master**
Three Cheers for September 1–2, SV 9836-1

Owls

 Owls are birds of prey that have sharp talons for catching their prey and hooked beaks for tearing it apart.

 The characteristics of owls are large heads, flat faces, forward-directed eyes, hooked beaks, strong legs, sharp claws, and soft feathers.

 There are two families of owls that live in North America. They are the barn owls and the typical owls.

 The barn owls have small eyes, a heart-shaped facial disk, long and slender legs, and white undersides. Barn owls do not hoot but make a variety of screeching sounds.

 Typical owls have large eyes, a rounded face, two tufts of head feathers resembling ears or horns, and dark undersides.

 Most owls are nocturnal, but several, including the burrowing owl, are active during the day.

 Most owls have excellent eyesight during the day as well as at night. Their eyes do not move in their sockets. They have to move their entire head, which has a range of about 270°, to look around.

 The owl's ear openings are behind and to the side of the eyes and provide an acute sense of hearing.

 Because owls have soft feathers, they can sneak up on their prey silently. Owls eat rodents, insects, frogs, fish, and birds.

 Owls eat smaller prey whole and larger prey in chunks. They cough up parts that cannot be digested such as hair, fur, and bones in oval-shaped pellets.

Three Cheers for September 1–2, SV 9836-1

Owl Puppets

Materials

- patterns on page 51
- brown lunch sacks
- brown, black, and yellow construction paper
- scissors
- glue
- circle stencil (2½ inches in diameter)
- circle stencil (2 inches in diameter)
- brown pipe cleaners

Directions

Teacher Preparation: Duplicate the wing, beak, and tuft patterns to use as templates. Provide a lunch sack for each child.

1. Trace and cut out two wings and tuft patterns on brown construction paper.

2. Turn the lunch sack upside down. Then glue the tuft pattern on the bottom flap of the sack and the wings on each side.

3. Trace two large circles on yellow construction paper. Cut them out and glue them on the bottom flap of the lunch sack so that they overlap the tuft pattern.

4. Trace two small circles on black construction paper. Cut them out and glue them on top of the yellow circles to make the pupils of the eyes.

5. Trace and cut out the beak pattern on yellow construction paper. Glue it below the eyes.

6. Cut and bend two short pieces of brown pipe cleaners for each of the owl's legs and talons. Poke them through the lower edge of the lunch sack. Twist the ends to secure them to the sack.

Owl Magnets

Materials

- orange juice can lids
- white paper
- wiggly eyes
- markers
- scissors
- glue
- magnetic tape
- spray paint

Directions

Teacher Preparation: Spray paint the rimmed side of the lids.

1. Trace the shape of the lid on the paper and cut it out.

2. Draw the head, the body, feet, and wings of an owl with markers on the paper.

3. Glue two wiggly eyes on the owl.

4. Glue the picture inside the rimmed edge of the lid. Trim to fit.

5. Cut a one-inch piece of magnetic tape and stick it to the back of the lid.

6. Use to hold any favorite papers on a metal surface.

Edible Owl Pellets

You will need

- 1 cup creamy peanut butter
- 2 tablespoons honey
- ⅔ cup dry milk
- 1 tablespoon raisins
- 1 tablespoon hard shell chocolate candies
- 1 tablespoon chocolate chips
- 1 tablespoon cinnamon hard candies
- mixing bowl and spoon
- measuring cups and spoons
- wax paper

Directions

Lead a discussion with children about owl pellets. See page 42 for teacher information.

See page 42 for teacher information.

1. Measure and mix together the peanut butter and honey in the mixing bowl.

2. Measure and stir in the dry milk. Knead until thoroughly mixed.

3. Stir in remaining ingredients until well-mixed.

4. Divide mixture and make twelve smooth, elongated balls. Recipe can be doubled.

5. Chill in the refrigerator.

Use with "What Did the Owl Eat?" on page 47 before eating, if desired.

Use with "What Did the Owl Eat?" on page 47 before eating, if desired.

Note: Be aware of any allergies that children may have.

Three Cheers for September 1–2, SV 9836-1

♫ Three Little Owls

(Tune: "Six Little Ducks")

Three little owls sat next to each other.

They were alone and missed their mother.

"I want my mommy," said the littlest one.

Then she flew back when night was done.

Have children learn this song to go along with "Owl Babies" on page 50.

Who-o-o Can Read These Books About Owls?

All About Owls
by Jim Arnosky (Scholastic)

The Barn Owl (Animal Lives)
by Sally Tagholm (Kingfisher)

Good-night, Owl
by Pat Hutchins (Aladdin)

Owl Babies
by Martin Waddell (Candlewick Press)

Owls
by Floyd Scholz (Stackpole)

Owly
by Mike Thaler (Walker & Company)

Welcome to the World of Owls
by Diane Swanson (Whitecap Books)

Three Cheers for September 1–2, SV 9836-1

"Whoos" the Wisest Owl?

Materials

- patterns on page 51
- craft paper
- brown, yellow, and black construction paper
- 6-inch paper plates
- scissors
- glue
- circle stencil (2½ inches in diameter)
- circle stencil (2 inches in diameter)
- brown pipe cleaners
- stapler
- brown paint
- sponges
- border

Directions

Teacher Preparation: Duplicate a copy of the wing, beak, and tuft to use as a template. Cover the bulletin board with craft paper.

1. Staple two paper plates together to form the head and body of the owl and sponge paint them brown.

2. Trace and cut out two wings and a tuft on brown construction paper.

3. Glue the tuft on the top of the head and the wings on each side of the body.

4. Trace two large circles on yellow construction paper. Cut them out and glue them on the head so that they slightly overlap the tuft pattern.

5. Trace two small circles on black construction paper. Cut them out and glue them on top of the yellow circles to make the pupils of the eyes.

6. Trace and cut out the beak pattern on yellow construction paper. Glue it below the eyes.

7. Cut and bend two short pieces of the brown pipe cleaners for each of the owl's talons. Staple them to the bottom edge of the body.

8. Arrange and staple the owls on the board in a pleasing arrangement and add a border and the caption.

Three Cheers for September 1–2, SV 9836-1

Owl Centers

Math Center

Math Standard
Answers questions using information organized in bar-type graphs

What Did the Owl Eat?

Materials

- activity master on page 52
- crayons
- toothpicks
- edible owl pellets made in "Edible Owl Pellets" on page 44
- paper plates

Teacher Preparation: Duplicate a copy of the activity master for each child. Prepare owl pellets and chill them in the refrigerator.

Lead a discussion with children about owl pellets. See page 42 for teacher information. Invite children to use a toothpick to break apart a peanut butter owl pellet to discover what is inside. Have them record on the graph the number of pieces of each food item that were in the pellet. Then have children use the results to answer the questions.

Language Center

Language Arts Standard
Produces rhyming words

Nice Mice

Materials

- patterns on page 53
- crayons or markers
- 2 wooden clothespins
- construction paper
- scissors
- glue

Teacher Preparation: Duplicate on construction paper two copies of the owl pattern and twelve copies of the mouse pattern. Color and cut them out. Glue a clothespin on the back of each owl pattern. Write a different rhyming word on the back of each mouse pattern.

Invite partners to spread the mice out on the table. Then have one child use an owl to "catch" a mouse with the clothespin. Have the child read the word on the back of the mouse and say another word that rhymes with it. Have the partner repeat the action. Encourage partners to continue playing until all of the mice are caught.

Owl Centers

Science Center

Science Standard
Demonstrates safe practices
during classroom investigations

Take a Closer Look

Materials

- owl pellets
- tweezers
- large resealable plastic bag
- latex gloves
- magnifying glass

Teacher Preparation: Look on page 42 for teacher information on owl pellets. Order inexpensive owl pellets online at www.sciencestuff.com. These pellets have been baked to kill any live bacteria, but safety precautions should be taken to protect children who may be allergic to birds. It is recommended to soak the pellets until they are completely wet to prevent any part of the pellet from being airborne. You may wish to take apart the pellets in a large group and discuss with children what was found. Then place the dissected pellet in a plastic bag for children to examine at the science table.

Invite children to use the magnifying glass to examine the bones and fur that were found in the owl pellet.

Writing Center

Language Arts Standard
Uses basic capitalization
and punctuation

Watching for Owls

Materials

- activity master on page 54
- crayons

Teacher Preparation: Duplicate a copy of the activity master for each child.

Invite children to color the owl and write each sentence correctly using capital letters and periods.

Owl Centers

Social Studies Center

Social Studies Standard
Uses a problem-solving process

Where's My Dinner?

Materials

• activity master on page 55

Teacher Preparation: Duplicate a copy of the activity master for each child.

Invite children to help the owl solve his problem by finding his dinner on the grid. Have them write the correct letter in each box.

Technology Center

Technology Standard
Applies keyword searches to acquire information

Owls Online

Materials

• computer with Internet access

• writing paper

Challenge children to find three facts about owls by doing a keyword search on the Internet. Have them write the facts on paper and share them with a partner.

Owl Centers

Physical Development Center

Physical Education Standard
Demonstrates an awareness of personal and general space

The Owl Catches the Mice

Materials

• a book about owls or birds of prey

Lead a discussion with children about owls being birds of prey. Invite one or two children to stand in the middle of a large space and pretend to be owls. Have remaining children stand around the edge and pretend to be mice. At a designated a signal, have the "mice" run to the other side of the area and have the "owls" try to tag the "mice." Children are out of the game when they are tagged. Repeat until all of the "mice" are tagged.

Literacy Center

Language Arts Standard
Retells or acts out the order of important events in a story

Owl Babies

Materials

• *Owl Babies* by Martin Waddell
• markers
• scissors
• white construction paper
• magnetic tape
• magnetic board

Teacher Preparation: Use construction paper to draw and cut out simple pictures of a mother owl and three baby owls. Make one of the baby owls smaller than the other two. Stick a small piece of magnetic tape on each owl.

Read to children or have children read *Owl Babies*. Reread so that they become familiar with the story. Lead a discussion with children about the characters in the story. Then invite them to retell the important events using the magnetic board. Encourage children to learn the song in "Three Little Owls" on page 45.

Wing, Beak, and Tuft Patterns

Use with "Owl Puppets" on page 43 and "'Whoos' the Wisest Owl?" on page 46.

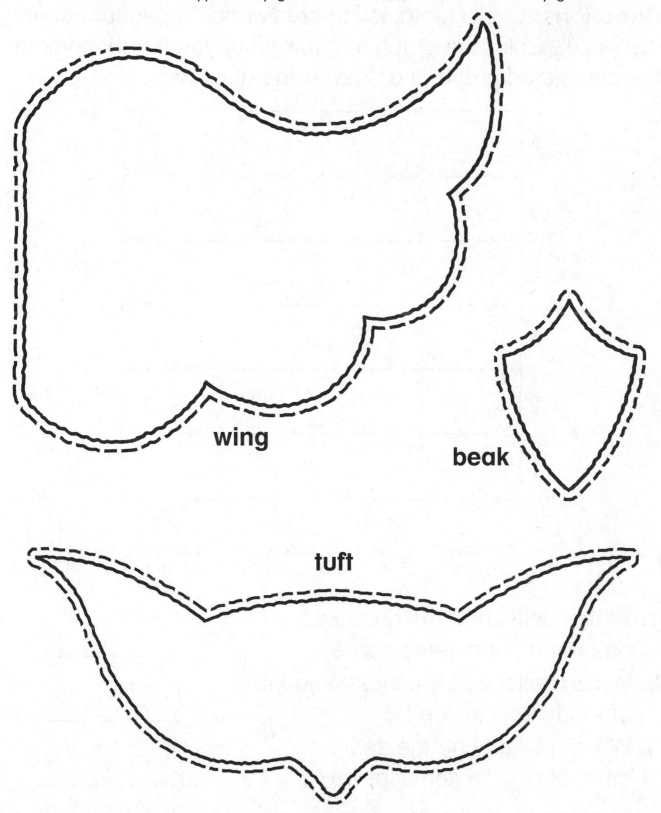

wing

beak

tuft

Owl Pellet Graph

Directions: Use a toothpick to break apart a peanut butter owl pellet. Color the graph to show what you found. Look at the completed graph and answer the questions.

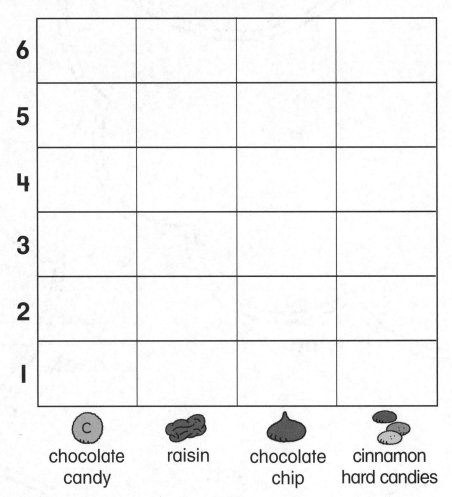

1. Which pellet had the greatest amount of food items inside? _____

2. Which pellet had the least amount of food items inside? _____

3. Which pellets had the same amount of food items inside? _____

Use with "What Did the Owl Eat?" on page 47.

Owl and Mouse Patterns

Use with "Nice Mice" on page 47.

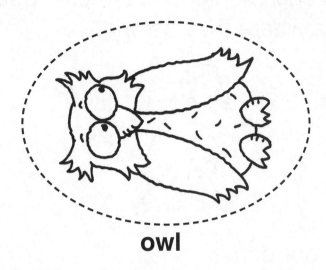

owl

mice

53

Name _____ **Date** _____

Writing

Directions: Write each sentence correctly. Use capital letters and periods where they belong.

1. i saw an owl in our barn

_____

_____

2. the owl made a screeching sound

_____

_____

3. then it flew quietly away

_____

_____

4. owls look for food at night

_____

_____

Use with "Watching for Owls" on page 48.

Find the Mice

Directions: Start at 0. Follow the directions. Which mouse is at that point? Write the letter.

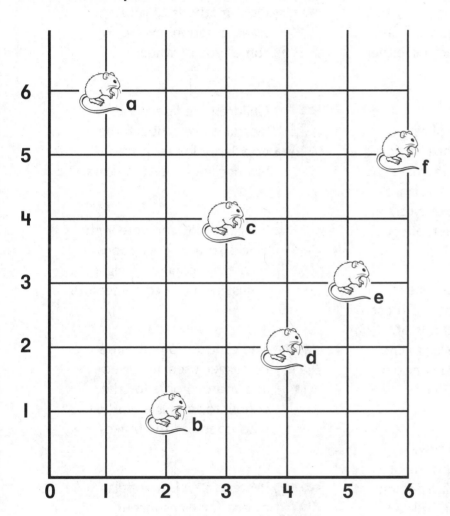

	Right	Up	Letter		Right	Up	Letter
1.	→ 2	↑ 1	☐	**4.**	→ 3	↑ 4	☐
2.	→ 1	↑ 6	☐	**5.**	→ 5	↑ 3	☐
3.	→ 4	↑ 2	☐	**6.**	→ 6	↑ 5	☐

Use with "Where's My Dinner?" on page 49.

Transportation Facts

 Transportation is a way to get people or goods from one point to another either by air, land, or water.

 Some methods of air transportation are powered by engines that increase the speed of travel. Airplanes, jets, and helicopters rely on engines to make them go.

 Airline travel remains one of the safest and most convenient methods of traveling. However, airline travel does raise concern about air pollution.

 Hot air balloon travel is not a practical means of transportation if a person is in a hurry. The balloon depends entirely on the speed of the wind, and there is no way to steer or control the direction that it goes.

 Most methods of land transportation involve some type of wheel.

 Children are fascinated by trains even though the popularity for train travel has declined over the years.

 Freight trains compete with trucks to transport goods across the country. Freight trains are more cost effective.

 The caboose on a train is no longer used. It served as a motor home for the conductor and the worker who operated the brakes.

 Water travel is a popular means for transporting passengers and cargo. In many instances, there is no other means of transportation to cross large bodies of water.

Three Cheers for September 1–2, SV 9836-1

A Butter Tub Sailboat

Materials

- patterns on page 65
- brown and white construction paper
- empty butter tubs with lids
- straws
- hole punch
- stapler
- scissors

Directions

Teacher Preparation: Duplicate the sail and boat patterns to use as a template. Enlarge to fit the size of butter tub used. Punch a hole in the center of each lid so that a straw can be inserted through the lid.

1. Trace and cut out a sail on white construction paper and two boats on brown construction paper.

2. Staple the two boat cutouts together at one end. Then wrap the cutouts around the butter tub. Staple the remaining ends together so that the paper fits snuggly around the tub.

3. Place the lid on top of the butter tub.

4. Hole punch a hole at the top and one at the bottom of the straight side of the sail. Put the straw through the holes for the mast of the sailboat.

5. Insert the bottom end of the straw through the hole in the lid to make the sail stand straight.

Shoe Box Train

Materials

- empty shoe boxes
- construction paper
- tempera paint
- paintbrushes
- black poster board
- plastic lids for wheel templates
- brads
- scissors
- glue
- sharpened pencil
- newspaper

Directions

Teacher Preparation: Punch small holes in the lower corners of both sides of the shoe boxes. This will be where the wheels will be attached.

1. Paint the outside of the shoe box a desired color. Allow it to dry.

2. Use the plastic lids to trace four circles on the black poster board for the train wheels. Cut them out. Younger children may need help cutting out the poster board.

3. Lay the circles on a thick section of newspaper. Carefully, use the sharpened pencil to poke a hole in the center of each circle. Younger children may need help.

4. For each circle, insert a brad through the hole. Then insert the brad through the hole in the shoe box to attach the "wheel" to the train car. Separate the prongs so that wheels can turn.

5. Be creative and use the construction paper to make the shoe box train car look like an engine or a caboose. Roll pieces of construction paper and glue the ends to make logs to put in the train car.

Cheesy Sailboats

You will need

- English muffins
- pimento cheese spread
- triangle-shaped tortilla chips
- plastic knives
- plates
- fork
- tablespoon

Directions

Teacher Preparation: Separate English muffins with a fork. Provide each child with half of an English muffin, a tablespoon of cheese spread, and two triangle-shaped tortilla chips.

1. Spread pimento cheese evenly over the muffin to cover.

2. Stand two tortilla chips in the cheese spread to look like the sails on a boat.

Extension: Have children write sentences to describe the steps used to make the sailboats.

♫ By Air, Land, or Water Song

(Tune: "Twinkle, Twinkle Little Star")

Ride a car or ride a train.

Ride a boat or ride a plane.

Ride a bike or ride a bus.

These are things that transport us.

Ride a helicopter way up high.

Or ride a rocket to the sky.

Traveling Tales

Airport
by Byron Barton (HarperTrophy)

All Aboard Airplanes
by Frank Evans (Grosset & Dunlap)

Alphabeep: A Zipping, Zooming ABC
by Debora Pearson (Holiday House)

Big Book of Trains
by Christine Heap (DK Publishing)

Curious George and the Hot Air Balloon
by H.A. and Margret Rey (Houghton Mifflin)

I Love Trucks
by Philemon Sturges (HarperCollins)

The Best Book of Trains
by Richard Balkwill (Kingfisher)

Trains, Planes, and Things That Go
by Todd South (Silver Dolphin)

Wings, Wheels, and Sails
by Bobbie Kalman (Crabtree Publishing Company)

Materials

- pattern on page 65
- scissors
- stapler
- craft paper
- yellow construction paper
- watercolor paints
- paintbrushes
- markers
- paper plates
- yarn
- border

Directions

Teacher Preparation: Duplicate the basket pattern on construction paper. Enlarge if desired. Provide a copy for each child. Cover bulletin board with craft paper.

1. Decorate the paper plate with watercolors to look like a hot air balloon.

2. Cut out the basket pattern. Write a word or a sentence telling what you might see from a hot air balloon.

3. Cut two six-inch lengths of yarn. Staple one end of each yarn piece to the paper plate.

4. Staple the other end of each yarn piece to the top of the basket.

5. Arrange and staple the hot air balloons in a pleasing arrangement on the bulletin board.

6. Add a border and the caption.

Three Cheers for September 1–2, SV 9836-1

By Air, Land, or Water Centers

Language Center

Language Arts Standard
Reads rhyming words

A Race to the Finish

Materials

- pattern on page 66
- 2 toy race cars
- number cube
- file folder
- glue

Teacher Preparation: Duplicate two copies of the game board pattern. Glue them on the file folder to form a racetrack. Write the word *START* on one section of the racetrack. Then laminate and write a sight word in each section of the game board. The board can be cleaned off and other words such as blends, digraphs, or compound words can be written on the board.

Invite partners to choose a race car marker and place it on *START*. Have them roll the number cube and drive the car the corresponding number of spaces. Then have children read the word on the space on which their car lands. They must read the word correctly in order to stay on that space. If they read the word incorrectly, they return to their previous space. Encourage children to continue playing until each player has finished the race.

Science Center

Science Standard
Understands that it is helpful to work with a team in science and share findings

Making the Boat Float

Materials

- foil
- plastic tub with water
- 20–30 pennies
- newspaper

Teacher Preparation: Cover the science table with newspaper and place the tub of water on the paper.

Have children work in groups. Invite them to each make a boat using the foil. Then have them put their boat on the water to make sure that it floats. Have them place pennies on their boat to see how many pennies it will hold before it sinks. Encourage children to compare their results with others in the group.

By Air, Land, or Water Centers

Math Center

Math Standard
Describes time on a clock using hour and half-hour

Airplane Arrival Times

Materials

- activity master on page 67
- crayons

Teacher Preparation: Duplicate a copy of the activity master for each child.

Invite children to write the flight number below the clock that shows the time that the plane arrives.

Communication Center

Language Arts Standard
Uses vocabulary to describe experiences

My Favorite Trip

Materials

- photographs or pictures from magazines of vacation destinations

Invite children to bring a photograph or picture from a magazine of a favorite place that they have visited or would like to visit. Have them share with the class something that they liked about that place. Then have them tell what means of transportation they used or would use to get there.

By Air, Land, or Water Centers

Social Studies Center

Social Studies Standard
Understands the need for rules and laws

Obey the Traffic Signs

Materials

- patterns on page 68
- scissors
- glue
- construction paper
- crayons or markers

Teacher Preparation: Duplicate patterns in order to have two of each traffic sign. Color and cut out the pictures. Glue them on construction paper, cut them to fit, and laminate.

Lead a discussion with children about the necessity for traffic signs in order to make traveling safe. Invite children to find the pairs of signs that match. Then have them tell what each sign means.

Game Center

Math Standard
Applies and adapts a variety of strategies to solve problems

Driving Home

Materials

- pattern on page 69
- crayons or markers
- washable markers
- paper towels
- file folder
- glue
- squirt bottle filled with water

Teacher Preparation: Duplicate a copy of the maze pattern. Color background pictures on the maze. Then glue the maze to the inside of a file folder and laminate.

Have children use washable markers to trace a path to help the car get to the house. Encourage children to spray and wipe the game board when they are finished.

By Air, Land, or Water Centers

Writing Center

All Kinds of Transportation

Materials

- activity master on page 70
- crayons or markers

Teacher Preparation: Duplicate a copy of the activity master for each child.

Invite children to write each sentence, leaving the correct spaces between the words. Encourage children to color the pictures.

Physical Development Center

Red Light, Green Light

Materials

- none

Teacher Preparation: Locate a large area inside or outside to play this game.

Invite one child to be the "traffic cop" and the remaining children to be the cars. Have the traffic cop turn around facing away from remaining children. Have an adult or teacher say, "Green Light," which signals children to run across the space and try to get to the opposite side. Then say, "Red Light," which signals the traffic cop to quickly turn around to see which cars are "speeding." Have the traffic cop send any "cars" that he or she sees moving to go back and start again. The remaining "cars" can continue play from where they stopped. Continue play until all "cars" reach the other side.

Sail and Boat Patterns

Use with "A Butter Tub Sailboat" on page 57.

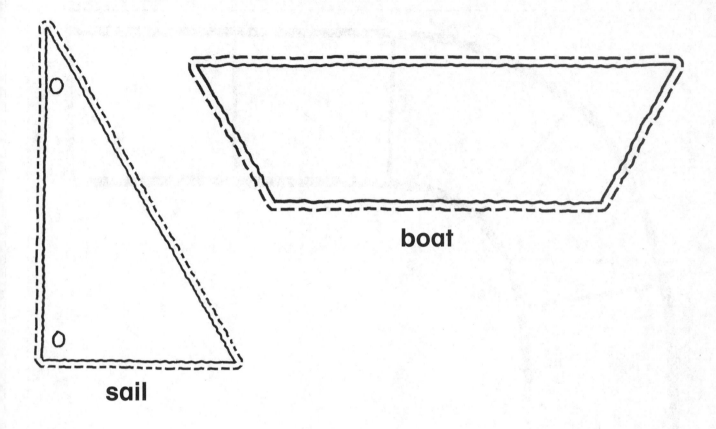

boat

sail

Basket Pattern

Use with "Up, Up, and Away" on page 60.

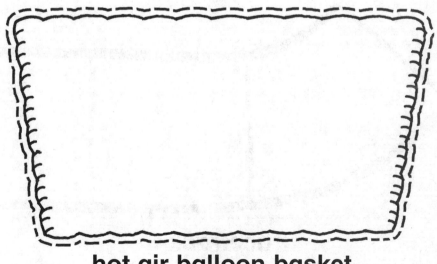

hot air balloon basket

Racetrack Pattern

Use with "A Race to the Finish" on page 61.

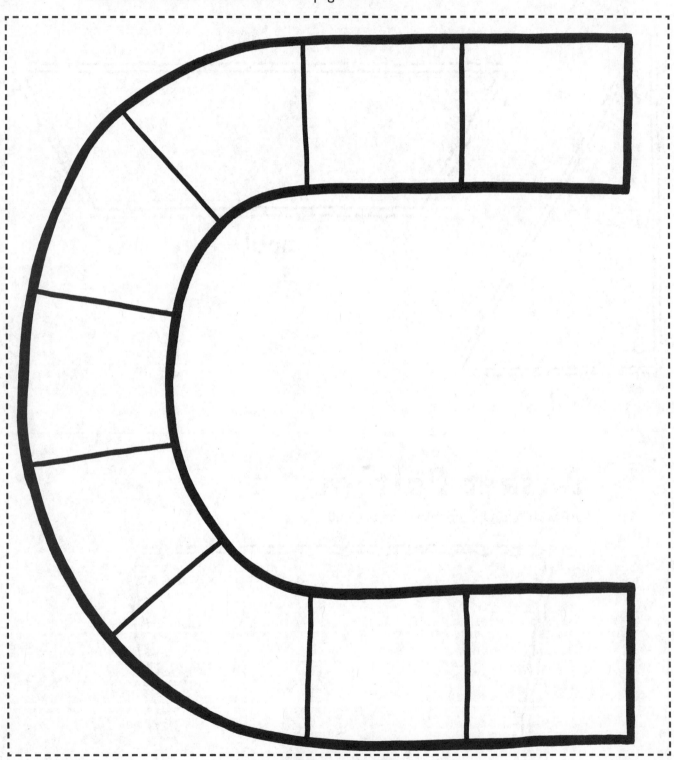

racetrack

Unit 5, By Air, Land, or Water: Pattern

Three Cheers for September 1–2, SV 9836-1

Arrival Times

Directions: Write the flight number below the clock that shows the time that the plane arrives.

Arrival Times	
Flight 23	2:00
Flight 16	3:30
Flight 41	10:30
Flight 102	4:00
Flight 37	12:30
Flight 54	9:30

1.

Flight _____

2.

Flight _____

3.

Flight _____

4.

Flight _____

5.

Flight _____

6.

Flight _____

Use with "Airplane Arrival Times" on page 62.

Traffic Sign Patterns
Use with "Obey the Traffic Signs" on page 63.

stop sign

one-way sign

railroad crossing sign

no bicycles sign

no right turn sign

speed limit sign

yield sign

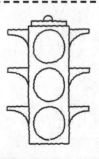

traffic light sign

Car Maze Pattern

Use with "Driving Home" on page 63.

Three Cheers for September 1–2, SV 9836-1

Name _____ **Date** _____

Writing Sentences

Directions: Write each sentence correctly.

1. Carshavefourwheels.

_____.

2. Trainsmoveontracks.

_____.

3. Planesflyhighandfast.

_____.

4. Boatsfloatonwater.

_____.

Use with "All Kinds of Transportation" on page 64.

Unit 5, By Air, Land, or Water: Activity Master
Three Cheers for September 1–2, SV 9836-1

Apple Facts

 Apples are part of the rose family.

 The state of Washington grows the most apples in the United States.

 There are over 7,500 different kinds of apples in the world.

 Apples have five seeds.

 An apple cut in half across its core will have a symmetrical star shape.

 The freshest apples can float because 25 percent of their volume is air.

 One tree produces enough apples to fill 20 boxes that weigh nearly 42 pounds each. That's twenty bushels of apples!

 John Chapman became known as Johnny Appleseed. He spent nearly 49 years walking around Ohio and Indiana planting and caring for apple orchards.

 The largest apple ever picked weighed over three pounds.

 It takes two pounds of apples to make one nine-inch apple pie.

 A bushel of apples will produce 20–24 quarts of applesauce.

 It takes 36 apples to make one gallon of cider.

 On October 16, 1976, Kathy Wafler Madison, at the age of 16, created the world's longest apple peel. It was 172 feet, 4 inches long. Madison later worked as a sales manager for an apple tree nursery.

Unit 6, Apples Aplenty: Teacher Information
Three Cheers for September 1–2, SV 9836-1

Apple Core Mobile

Materials

- patterns on page 80
- red and white construction paper
- brown yarn
- black marker
- scissors
- glue

Directions

Teacher Preparation: Duplicate the apple core patterns to use as a template.

1. Trace the top and bottom apple templates on red construction paper. Trace and cut out four pieces.

2. Trace the core template on white construction paper. Make two core pieces and cut them out. Use black marker to draw seeds.

3. Cut a one-foot piece of yarn.

4. Arrange a top, a center, and a bottom facedown on a flat surface. Lay the piece of yarn across the three sections allowing the yarn to hang freely from the top as the stem. Glue yarn to apple core pieces.

5. Glue the matching pieces together with the yarn between the pieces.

6. Hang from the ceiling.

Stand-up Apple Tree

Materials

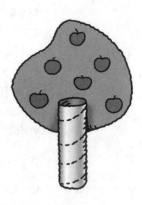

- empty bathroom tissue rolls
- green construction paper
- red paint
- pink tissue paper
- one-inch corks
- scissors
- pencil
- glue

Directions

Teacher Preparation: Cut a two-inch slit on each side of one end of the tissue rolls. Cut tissue paper into one-inch squares.

1. Fold the construction paper in half like a book. Draw the top part of a tree making it as big as possible.

2. Cut out the tree on the folded paper, resulting in two trees that match.

3. Dip the end of the cork in the red paint and cover one paper tree with apple prints.

4. Twist and glue the pink tissue paper squares on the other tree to represent apple blossoms.

5. Glue the two tree cutouts together to make a double thickness. One side has apples and the other side has blossoms.

6. Gently slide the tree into the slits on the tissue roll to make the tree stand.

A-peeling Applesauce

You will need

- 6 medium apples (1 apple = ½ cup applesauce)
- 1 cup water
- ½ cup sugar
- ½ teaspoon cinnamon
- saucepan
- plastic knives
- paring knife
- measuring spoons and cups
- hot plate
- potato masher or blender
- paper bowls
- plastic spoons

Directions

Teacher Preparation: Wash the apples thoroughly. For younger children, peel and core the apples ahead of time.

1. Peel, core, and cut up the apples. Leave the peels on for pink applesauce.

2. Place in a saucepan with water, sugar, and cinnamon.

3. Cook uncovered for about 40 minutes until apples are soft enough to mash. A microwave oven or crock pot can be used if a hot plate is not available.

4. Mash or blend the apples for desired consistency.

5. Chill and serve.

Note: Save the seeds from the apples to use for making apple shakers in "Shake, Shake, Shake!" on page 77.

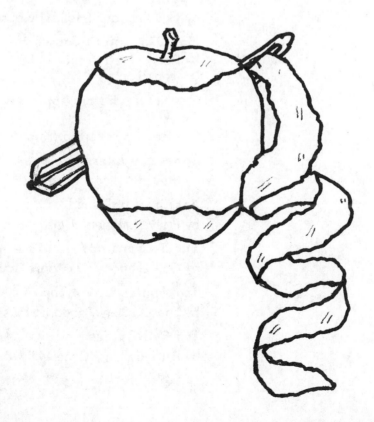

Apples Aplenty

Apples aplenty
Apples galore,
I can't get enough,
I always want more.
Red apples, yellow apples, green apples, too.
They're juicy and crunchy
And so good for you!

Books Worth Biting Into . . .

Apples
by Gail Gibbons (Holiday House)

How Do Apples Grow?
by Betsy Maestro and Giulio Maestro
(HarperTrophy)

How to Make an Apple Pie and See the World
by Marjorie Priceman (Knopf)

Johnny Appleseed
by Steven Kellogg (Scholastic)

Johnny Appleseed
by Reeve Lindbergh (Little, Brown and Company)

The Seasons of Arnold's Apple Tree
by Gail Gibbons (Harcourt Brace and Jovanovich)

Ten Apples Up on Top
by Theo LeSieg (Random House)

Ten Red Apples
by Pat Hutchins (Greenwillow)

Three Cheers for September 1–2, SV 9836-1

The Seasons of the Apple Tree

Materials

- blue craft paper
- large manila paper
- crayons
- white chalk
- green paint
- red dot stickers
- pencil with unused eraser
- pink tissue paper
- scissors
- glue
- border
- stapler

Directions

Teacher Preparation: Cover the bulletin board with blue craft paper. Cut manila paper in half lengthwise. Cut tissue paper into one-inch squares.

1. Fold the paper into quarters. Label each section Winter, Spring, Summer, and Fall.

2. Draw a brown tree trunk with branches in each of the four sections on the paper.

3. Draw snow on the first tree with the chalk for winter.

4. Draw green leaves on the second trunk. Twist and glue tissue squares on the tree for the blossoms in spring.

5. Dip the eraser end of the pencil in green paint and stamp circles on the third tree for the green apples in the summer.

6. Cover the fourth tree with red sticker dots for the red apples in the fall.

7. Arrange and staple children's work in a pleasing arrangement on the bulletin board. Add a border and the caption.

Unit 6, Apples Aplenty: Bulletin Board
Three Cheers for September 1–2, SV 9836-1

Apples Aplenty Centers

Math Center

Math Standard
Identifies and extends patterns to make predictions and solve problems

What's the Rule?

Materials

• activity master on page 81

• crayons

Teacher Preparation: Duplicate a copy of the activity master for each child.

Invite children to look at each row of apples for a pattern. Have them write two more numbers to complete the pattern. Then have them write the rule and color the apples.

Language Center

Language Arts Standard
Knows order of the alphabet

Alphabetical Apples

Materials

• patterns on page 80

• markers

• white construction paper

• scissors

Teacher Preparation: Duplicate on construction paper 26 apple patterns. Color and cut them out. Laminate for durability. Write one letter of the alphabet on each apple.

Invite children to lay the apples on the table in alphabetical order.

Extension: Write vocabulary words on several of the apples. Then have the children alphabetize the words.

Apples Aplenty Centers

Social Studies Center

Social Studies Standard
Identifies ordinary people who exemplify good citizenship

Johnny Appleseed

Materials

• a book about Johnny Appleseed
• activity master on page 82

Read to children one of the stories about Johnny Appleseed from the book list on page 74. Explain that John Chapman has become a legend for his kindness and generosity. Invite children to read the situations and write a sentence telling how they could be kind to their friends and family.

Music Center

Fine Arts Standard
Creates short rhythmic patterns

Shake, Shake, Shake!

Materials

• patterns on page 83
• scissors
• glue
• red, brown, and green construction paper
• stapler
• apple seeds from cooking activity in "A-peeling Applesauce" on page 73

Teacher Preparation: Duplicate the apple patterns for use as templates.

Invite children to trace and cut out two red apple shapes, one brown stem, and one green leaf. Then have them glue the stem to the top of one of the apples and glue the leaf (pointing upwards) to the bottom of the stem. Place a small amount of glue around the edge of the apple and place the other apple shape on top. Do not glue the flaps on the side. Allow the glue to dry. Put several apple seeds inside and fold in the flaps. Staple the edge closed. Encourage children to create rhythmic patterns as they shake, shake, shake.

Apples Aplenty Centers

Science Center

Language Arts Standard
Writes labels for charts

Parts of an Apple

Materials

- one apple with a stem
- crayons or markers
- paper
- knife

Teacher Preparation: Cut the apple in half, making sure that the stem remains.

Invite children to draw a picture of the inside of the apple. Then have them label the parts of the apple. Have them include these parts: skin, meat, seeds, core, and stem.

Game Center

Language Arts Standard
Knows final digraphs: *ch, sh, th*

The Ant Finds the Apple

Materials

- activity master on page 84
- crayons

Teacher Preparation: Duplicate a copy of the activity master for each child.

Invite children to help the ant find the apple by coloring the pictures that end in *ch, sh,* and *th.*

Apples Aplenty Centers

Literacy Center

Social Studies Standard
Retells stories from selected folktales

Fiction or Nonfiction

Materials

• story about Johnny Appleseed

Read to or have children read the story about Johnny Appleseed. Then invite them to retell the story to a friend. Encourage them to talk about a part of the story that could be true and a part that is probably make-believe.

Writing Center

Language Arts Standard
Composes complete sentences with correct punctuation

My Favorite Apple Food

Materials

• activity master on page 85
• crayons
• samples of various foods made from apples

Teacher Preparation: Duplicate a copy of the activity master for each child. Provide a taste sample of each food for children.

Invite children to taste different foods that are made from apples such as applesauce, apple pie, apple muffins, or apple juice. Then have them write a sentence telling about their favorite one and why they like it.

Apple Core Patterns

Use with "Apple Core Mobile" on page 72.

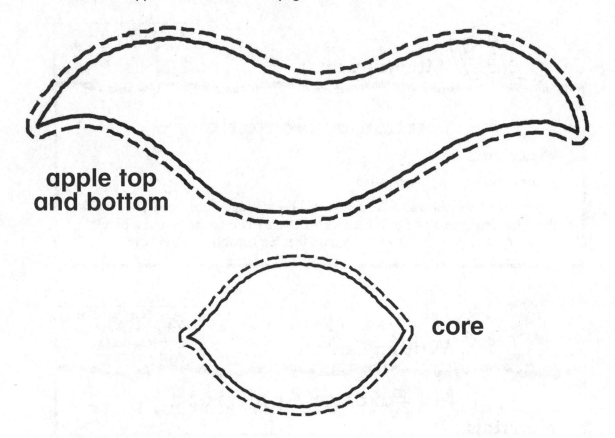

apple top
and bottom

core

Apple Patterns

Use with "Alphabetical Apples" on page 76.

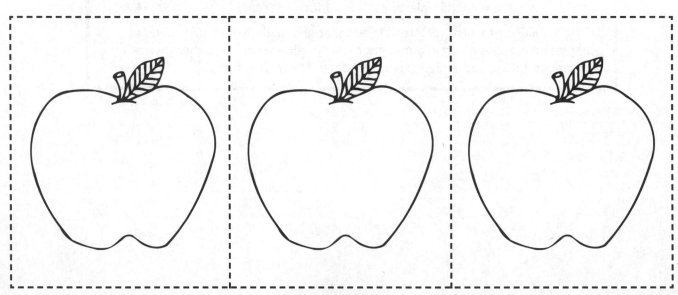

apples

Three Cheers for September 1–2, SV 9836-1

Name _____ **Date** _____

Find the Rule

Directions: Look for a pattern. Write two more numbers to complete the pattern. Then write the rule. Color the apples.

1.
 25 27 29 31

Rule:_____

2.
 44 41 38 35

Rule:_____

3.
 70 60 50 40

Rule:_____

4.
 25  50  75  100

Rule:_____

Use with "What's the Rule?" on page 76.

Name _____ Date _____

Being Kind

Directions: Read the sentences. Write what you would do to be kind.

1. You and your friend both want to play on the computer. What can you do?

   _____

   _____

2. Your friend has too many things to carry to the bus. What can you do?

   _____

   _____

3. Your mom rushes to get dinner on the table. What can you do?

   _____

   _____

4. Some children tease your friend on the playground. What can you do?

   _____

   _____

Use with "Johnny Appleseed" on page 77.

Unit 6, Apples Aplenty: Activity Master
Three Cheers for September 1–2, SV 9836-1

Apple Shaker Patterns

Use with "Shake, Shake, Shake!" on page 77.

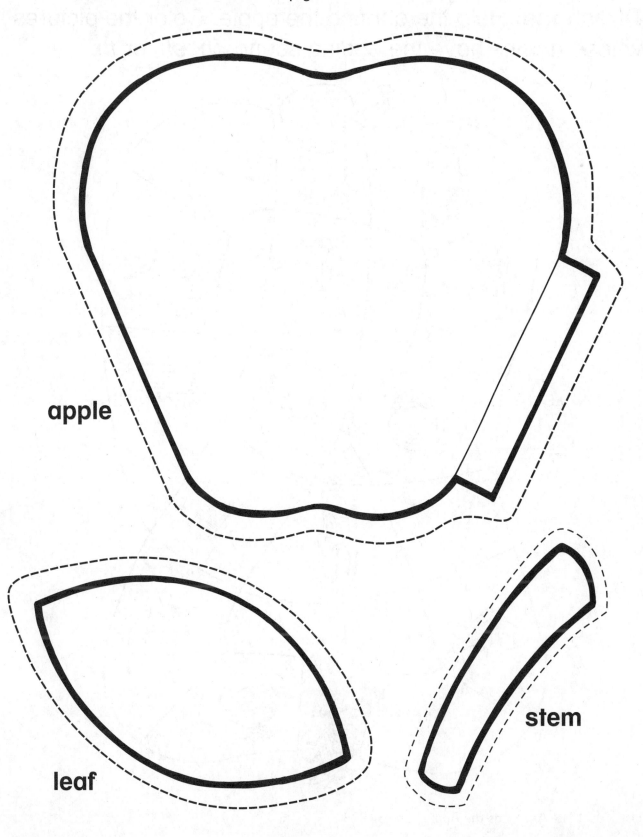

apple

leaf

stem

Ant and Apple Maze

Directions: Help the ant find the apple. Color the pictures whose names have the ending sound *ch*, *sh*, or *th*.

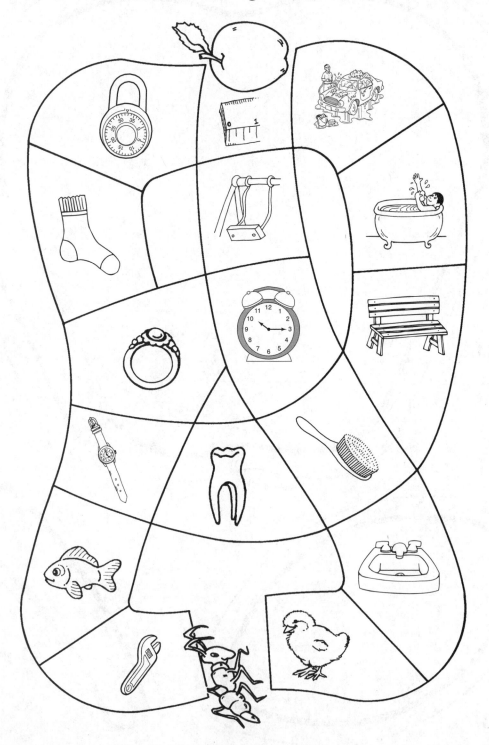

Use with "The Ant Finds the Apple" on page 78.

Name _____ **Date** _____

My Favorite Apple Recipe

Directions: Write a sentence about the apple food that you like the best. Tell why you like it.

Use with "My Favorite Apple Food" on page 79.

Three Cheers for September 1–2, SV 9836-1

A Look at H.A. and Margret Rey

 Hans Augusto Rey was born in Hamburg, Germany, on September 16, 1898. Margret Waldstein was also born there on May 16, 1906.

 After meeting briefly in Germany, Hans and Margret were reunited while working in Rio de Janeiro. They were married in 1935 and moved to Paris.

 It was there that their first book, *Cecily G. and the Nine Monkeys*, was published. It was about a giraffe and nine monkeys, including Curious George, who were friends in the jungle.

 The Reys were later convinced to write a story just about the antics of the curious monkey, George.

 It was at this time that Hitler was poised to take over Paris. The couple was forced to flee from Paris on bicycles with a handful of manuscripts (one of which starred Curious George).

 They soon made their way to New York City. In 1941, Houghton Mifflin published *Curious George* for the first time.

 Even though the Curious George books were a joint creation, the publisher suggested that the books would sell better if only H.A. Rey's name appeared on the books. The publisher said a male author would be unique because the children's book field was dominated by women at the time.

 After a time, Margret Rey rethought that decision and had her name included on the books.

 Hans broke barriers with his illustrations when he chose to include black children in his illustrations. This was relatively unheard of in the 1940's.

Unit 7, Author Study: Teacher Information
Three Cheers for September 1–2, SV 9836-1

Curious George
by H.A. and Margret Rey

A "George" Puppet

Materials

- patterns on page 90
- brown lunch sacks
- crayons or markers
- scissors
- glue
- construction paper
- craft items such as ribbon, yarn, and buttons

Directions

Teacher Preparation: Duplicate a copy of the monkey head and two arms for each child.

1. Color and cut out the head and arms of the monkey.

2. Turn the lunch sack upside down. Then glue the head pattern on the bottom flap of the sack and the arms on each side.

3. Use construction paper and craft items to create a new hat for George.

Curious George Word Puzzle

Materials

- activity master on page 91

Directions

Teacher Preparation: Duplicate a copy of the activity master for each child.

Invite children to read each word aloud. Then have them look at the shape of the boxes. Have them find a word that matches the shape and print the word in the boxes.

Books by H.A. and Margret Rey

- *Cecily G. and the Nine Monkeys* (Houghton Mifflin)

- *Curious George* (Houghton Mifflin)

- *Curious George and the Dumptruck* (Houghton Mifflin)

- *Curious George and the Firefighters* (Houghton Mifflin)

- *Curious George and the Rocket* (Houghton Mifflin)

- *Curious George at the Parade* (Houghton Mifflin)

- *Curious George Flies a Kite* (Houghton Mifflin)

- *Curious George Gets a Medal* (Houghton Mifflin)

- *Curious George Goes Fishing* (Houghton Mifflin)

- *Curious George Goes to School* (Houghton Mifflin)

- *Curious George Goes to the Hospital* (Houghton Mifflin)

- *Pretzel* (HarperCollins)

- *Whiteblack the Penguin Sees the World* (Houghton Mifflin)

Bookmark Patterns

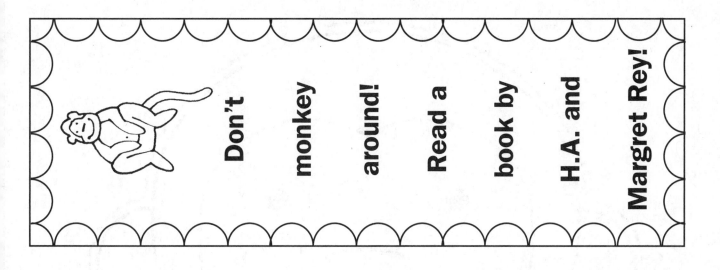

Don't monkey around! Read a book by H.A. and Margret Rey!

Reel in a good book by H.A. and Margret Rey!

Be curious! Read a book by H.A. and Margret Rey!

Three Cheers for September 1–2, SV 9836-1

Head and Arm Patterns

Use with "A 'George' Puppet" on page 87.

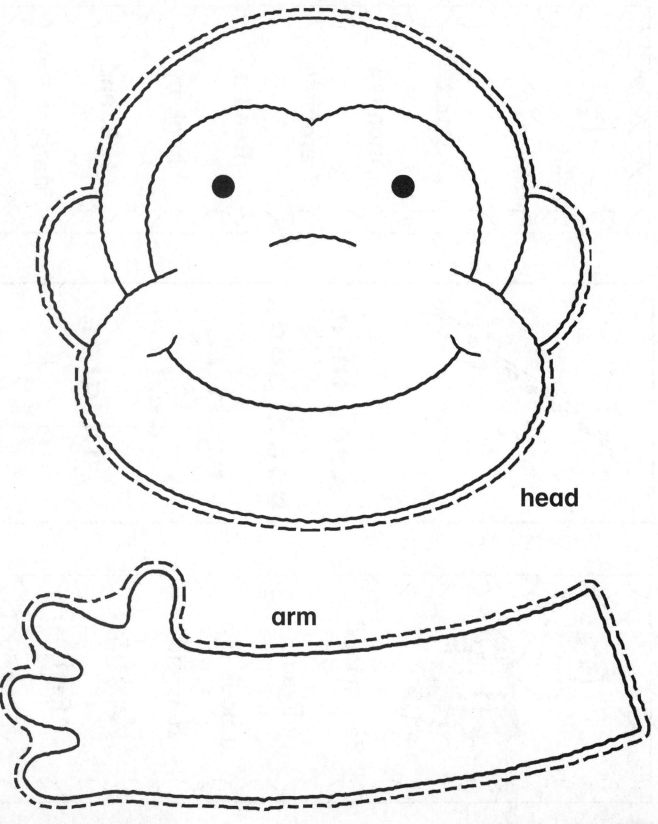

head

arm

Name _____ **Date** _____

"George" Word Puzzle

Directions: Read each word aloud. Find a word that matches the shape of the boxes. Print the word in the boxes.

monkey	yellow	jungle
friend	hat	

1.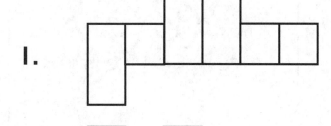

2.

3.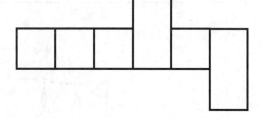

4.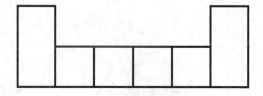

5.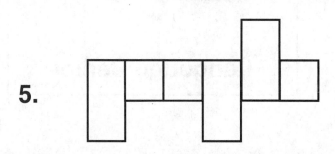

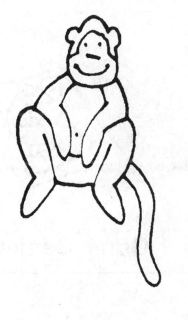

Use with "Curious George Word Puzzle" on page 87.

Unit 7, Author Study: Activity Master
Three Cheers for September 1–2, SV 9836-1

Center Icons Patterns

Art Center

Communication Center

Game Center

Language Center

Center Icons Patterns

Literacy Center

Math Center

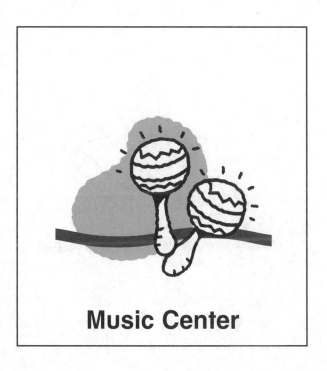

Music Center

Physical Development Center

Center Icons Patterns
Three Cheers for September 1–2, SV 9836-1

Center Icons Patterns

Science Center

Social Studies Center

Technology Center

Writing Center

Center Icons Patterns
Three Cheers for September 1–2, SV 9836-1

Student Awards

"Wh-o-o's" been a good worker?

_____

_____
Teacher's signature   Date

Congratulations, _____

You are the September
Student of the Month for

_____

_____
Teacher's signature   Date

Student Award

Congratulations!

_____ is chugging

right along in _____ .

_____   _____

Teacher's signature   **Date**

Calendar Day Pattern

Suggested Uses
- Reproduce the card for each day of the month. Write the numerals on each card and place it on your class calendar. Use cards to mark special days.
- Reproduce to make cards to use in word ladders or word walls.
- Reproduce to make cards and write letters on each card. Children use the cards to play word games forming words.
- Reproduce to make cards to create matching or concentration games for children to use in activity centers. Choose from the following possible matching skills or create your own:
    - uppercase and lowercase letters
    - pictures of objects whose names rhyme, have the same beginning or ending sounds, or contain short or long vowels
    - pictures of adult animals and baby animals
    - number words and numerals
    - numerals and pictures of objects
    - colors and shapes
    - high-frequency sight words